EDGWARE AND WILLESDEN TRAMWAYS

Robert J Harley

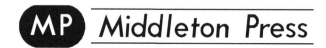

MP Middleton Press

Cover Picture: A late 1920s view of Paddington tram terminus reveals Metropolitan Electric Tramways c. 74. Note the motorman in his smart summer uniform. (G.N.Southerden)

Cover Colours: These reflect the livery applied to horsecars of the Harrow Road & Paddington Tramway Company.

This book is dedicated to the memory of
Dr.Hugh Nicol

Published July 1998

ISBN 1 901706 18 4

© Middleton Press 1998

Design Deborah Goodridge

Published by
Middleton Press
Easebourne Lane
Midhurst, West Sussex
GU29 9AZ
Tel: 01730 813169
Fax: 01730 812601

Printed & bound by Biddles Ltd,
Guildford and Kings Lynn

CONTENTS

INTRODUCTION AND ACKNOWLEDGEMENTS

This book completes the Tramway Classics coverage of the former lines of the Metropolitan Electric Tramways Company, known to all as the MET, with each letter pronounced separately. The routes from Edgware and Sudbury to Paddington, which formed the western half of the METs domain, are illustrated with the help of many photographers, past and present, whose names are listed with the captions. My gratitude goes to all those who have supplied views for inclusion in this book. I must single out Dave Jones and B.J. "Curly" Cross for particular mention as they have given of their time and collections so that all readers may enjoy a journey into the past. Thanks are also due to Terry Russell who kindly supplied the rolling stock drawings.

Readers wanting detailed information about the local tramways are directed to the two volume work on the MET written by Cyril Smeeton.

Many photographs used in the *Tramway Classics* series are the work of the late D.A.Thompson. Prints from the original negatives of these and many others not featured in the albums are available from the London County Council Tramways Trust. For further details please write to LCCTT, 66 Lady Somerset Road, Kentish Town, London, NW5 1TU. Enclosing a stamped addressed envelope. All proceeds go to further restoration of London Tramcars.

London Transport timetables and maps are reproduced by kind permission of LT Museum, Covent Garden.

GEOGRAPHICAL SETTING

Many of the north west suburbs of London experienced urban growth with the arrival of the tramways. Previous to this there were extensive tracts of open countryside and farmland. Much of the area was contained in the former County of Middlesex, which effectively ceased to exist in April 1965 when the Greater London Council was established. The Harrow Road eastwards from Kensal Green was situated in London County Council territory.

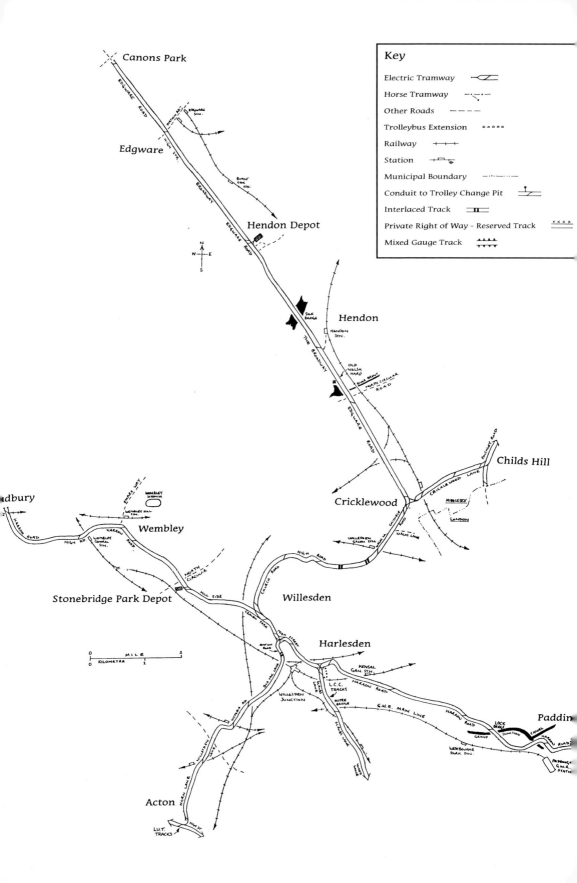

HISTORICAL BACKGROUND

The Harrow Road was first served by horse tramways belonging to the Harrow Road and Paddington Tramways Co.; opening date for the lines from Lock Bridge to Harlesden, with a short branch along Chippenham Road, was 7th July 1888. Traffic on the Chippenham Road branch did not live up to expectations, and this particular tramway backwater was later overlooked in the enthusiasm for electric traction which took hold of the area in the first decade of the twentieth century.

Electric lines promoted by the MET soon spread along the highways. On 3rd December 1904 the section from Cricklewood to Hendon Depot and Edgware opened; this was followed on 30th March 1906 by the route from Cricklewood to Willesden Green Station. Harlesden to Iron Bridge, Stonebridge Park commenced on 10th October 1906, with an extension from Harlesden along the Harrow Road to Lock Bridge coming into service on 22nd December of the same year. In the following year trams reached Canons Park from Edgware on 31st October, and at the end of 1907, on 23rd December, the section from Willesden Green to Craven Park was inaugurated. Activity in 1908 saw the Stonebridge Park line extended on 15th April to Wembley & Sudbury LNWR Station. On 30th May the LCC opened their tramway in Scrubs Lane, and this was later to form an important link to the LUT lines at Hammersmith and to the rest of the LCC system south of the River Thames. On 3rd June 1908 trams from Harlesden reached Willesden Junction, and this line finally opened for traffic to Acton on 8th October 1909. On 21st February 1910 the western lines were joined to the rest of the MET by a connection from Golders Green to Cricklewood. In the spring of 1910 a junction was put in with the LCC lines at College Park, Harlesden. Further progress on the Harrow Road resulted in the opening of the Paddington terminus on 6th December 1910. Previously, on 24th September, MET cars began to carry passengers from Wembley Station to the Swan at Sudbury. A connection between Metropolitan Electric and London United lines at Acton was installed in July 1915.

During the First World War many local industries benefitted by the frequent and reliable tram services which transported workers vital for the war effort. After the guns fell silent, the MET set about modernising its fleet and throughout the 1920s the quality of service was improved. The following local routes are listed in the 1929 map and guide:

30 Craven Park - Tooting Junction (LCC cars)
40 Whetstone - Cricklewood
54 Hendon - Willesden Green
60 North Finchley - Paddington
62 Sudbury - Paddington
66 Canons Park - Acton
68 Acton - Harlesden, Jubilee Clock

The establishment of the London Passenger Transport Board in 1933 put a big question mark over the retention and modernisation of tramways in the capital. Indeed, it was soon apparent that railed vehicles were out of favour and would shortly be replaced by trolleybuses. The conversion process began in July 1936 when routes 66 and 68 succumbed. Hendon Depot was used to scrap tramcars, but this ceased on 24th October 1936 when the tracks outside were abandoned. The last active section of western area MET track was converted in September 1937, when trams were removed from the Craven Park to Scrubs Lane section. Ironically the replacing trolleybuses were also later given short shrift by London Transport, and they disappeared in 1960-62, being replaced by diesel buses.

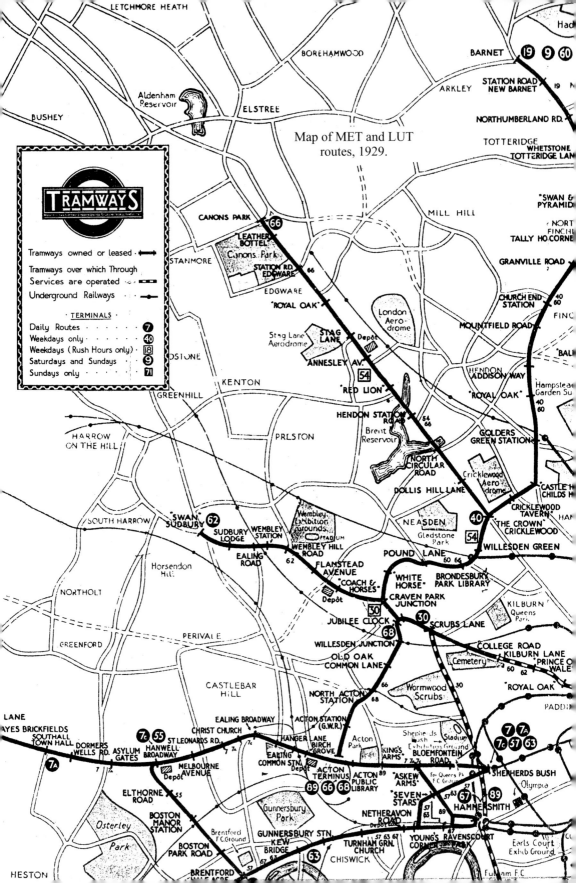

Map of MET and LUT
routes, 1929.

PASS DOWN THE CAR, PLEASE!

1. In many respects the dawn of the twentieth century coincided with a high water mark in British coachbuilding which imparted an air of durable elegance to the first electric tramcars. Let us first choose our transport of delight to explore the local tramways. If the weather is fine, what better than an outside seat on this splendid vehicle, car 106 - delivered new to the MET in 1905. Of course, no exhaust fumes will disturb

us, because this is a clean, environmentally friendly way of getting about.   (B.J.Cross Coll.)

2. If April showers threaten, then a seat on the front balcony of car 3 will give a bracing ride, with a canopy to offer some protection from the elements. We can also admire the artistry of the wrought iron tracery around our vantage point on the top deck.   (D.Jones Coll.)

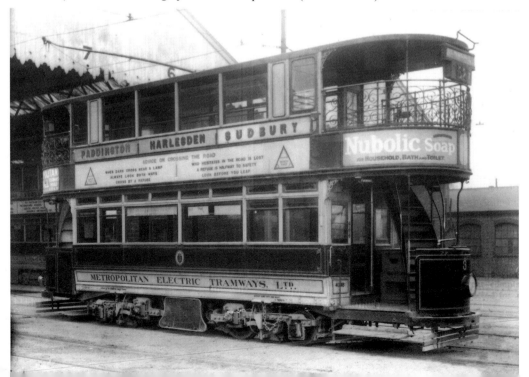

3. Our third choice of car indicates a desire to take a ride on this fine product supplied by the Brush Electrical Engineering Company of Loughborough. It may be inclement outside, but from the enclosed upper saloon we have a good view of London street life in the late Edwardian era. (Brush)

4. Many travellers seek other, like minded folk, and to join this party requires our best bib and tucker. The momentous occasion is the first electric tram to Willesden Green. At the helm is Alderman Nield of Middlesex County Council. We are in exalted company today, but where are all the ladies? Perhaps they are relaxing in the curtained seclusion of the lower saloon. (D.Jones Coll.)

5. We may prefer a more informal atmosphere on our voyage of discovery through an area where sunlit woodland glades have yet to give way to bricks and mortar. We join what is perhaps a church outing or a treat for family and friends of tramway employees. We are heading for a terminus on the edge of the countryside where we will leave the tram to find a suitable site for our picnic. (D.Jones Coll.)

CANONS PARK TO EDGWARE

6. It is the summer of 1936 and car 2497 rests in the evening sunshine at Canons Park terminus. That the rails were never extended beyond this point was not for want of trying by the MET. However, a powerful lobby of local residents effectively barred trams from encroaching on other parts of Stanmore. Arguments centred on class prejudice against a supposed influx of poorer "trippers" who would be inclined to make use of the cheap fares offered by the MET. So the end of the line remained just that, and even after trolleybus conversion, the wires did not get any further. (A.D.Packer)

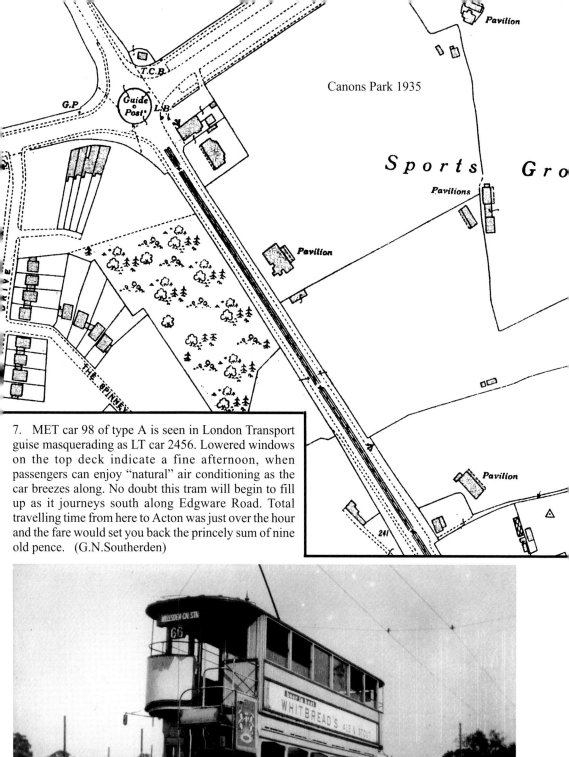

Canons Park 1935

7. MET car 98 of type A is seen in London Transport guise masquerading as LT car 2456. Lowered windows on the top deck indicate a fine afternoon, when passengers can enjoy "natural" air conditioning as the car breezes along. No doubt this tram will begin to fill up as it journeys south along Edgware Road. Total travelling time from here to Acton was just over the hour and the fare would set you back the princely sum of nine old pence. (G.N.Southerden)

8. Car 179 stands at the original (1904) Edgware terminus before the line was extended to Canons Park. Note the wonderful jumble of cottages which present a vista of English vernacular architecture at its most eccentric. B.J.Cross Coll.)

9. High Street, Edgware and the thirsty traveller has a choice of refreshment establishments. For those of a temperance disposition, car 84 will deliver you right outside the Bank Parade Tea Rooms. Passengers seeking something stronger should decamp across the road to the Masons Arms. Meanwhile, the carter in the centre of the picture takes advantage of the superior paving paid for by the tramway company. According to law, the MET had to maintain the road surface up to 18ins./ 46cms from the outer rail of each track. (B.J.Cross Coll.)

10. Car 2410 is a foreigner in these parts, having started out as London United car 261. It was top covered in 1928 and was referred to as type WT. Edgware now looks quite built up in this 1936 view, and after initial ribbon development caused by the arrival of the trams in 1904, the next real impetus for suburban housing was the opening of the "tube" (later called the Northern Line) in 1924. (A.D.Packer)

8 VICTORIA — PUTNEY — CRAVEN PARK

Via-Vauxhall Bridge, Wandsworth Rd., Clapham Junction, Wandsworth, Putney, Fulham Pal. Rd., Hammersmith, Shepherds Bush, Wormwood Scrubs, Nr. Willesden Junc., Harlesden, Extended to Wembley Ch., via Stonebridge Pk., Weekday rush hours. Operates Victoria—Harrow Rd. (Scrubs Lane) only, on Sundays.
Service interval, Victoria—Craven Pk., 5—8 mins. Craven Pk.—Wembley 10—12 mins.
Journey time, Victoria—Scrubs Lane 61 mins.—Craven Pk. 73 mins.—Wembley 87 mins.
Through fares, Vic.—Scrubs Lane 5d., Vic.—Craven Pk. 6d., Victoria—Wembley Church 9d.

	MON. to FRI.		SATURDAY		SUNDAY	
	First	Last	First	Last	First	Last
Victoria to Craven Park	6 2	6 29	10 54	6 2	6 29	10 54	......	....
Victoria to Harrow Road (Scrubs Lane)	6 2	6 29	11 2	6 2	6 29	11 8	8 25	11 15
Victoria to York Road	6 2	6 29	12 9	6 2	6 29	12 6	8 25	12 3
Craven Park to Victoria	6 41	6 47	10 56	6 41	6 47	10 56	......	....
Craven Park to Putney	6 41	6 47	12 5	6 41	6 47	12 8	......	....
Scrubs Lane to Victoria	6 25	6 31	11 2	6 25	6 31	11 2	9 26	11 0
Scrubs Lane to Putney	6 25	6 31	12 11	6 25	6 31	12 13	9 26	12 19
Clapham Junction to Victoria	5 35	6 4	11 44	5 35	6 4	11 46	8 4	11 41
Hammersmith to Victoria	5 39	5 47	11 19	5 39	5 47	11 18	7 40	11 16
Hammersmith to Clapham Junction	5 39	5 47	12 24	5 39	5 47	12 30	7 40	12 35
York Road to Wembley	5 50	6 0	8 10	5 29	5 50	8 20	......	....
York Road to Wembley ... afternoon	3 28	3 37	6 49	11 2	11 12	9 54	......	....
Wembley to York Road ... morning	6 27	6 38	9 7	6 27	6 38	9 17	......	....
Wembley to York Road ... afternoon	4 27	4 37	7 48	12 2	12 12	10 53	......	....

Edgware 1914

Rectory

Edgware Place

Purcell's Farm

S.D

MANNS ROAD

MANOR PARK CRESCENT

CHILTON ROAD

CHURCH LANE

186

Lodges

Lodge

Bank

184

Smy.

L.B

W.M

Railway Hotel

St. Margaret's Church
(Rectory)

Grave Yard

Sun. Sch.

P.O.

P.H.

G.P

MEADS ROAD

P.H.

Pol. Sta.

Institute

Congl. Chap.

Court Ho.

FERN SIDE

THORN BANK

HIGH STREET

F.E. Sta.

P.H.

Inn

Tr.

Smy.

G.P

P.

P.

11. A symmetrical arrangement of span wires and electric street lamps hangs above car 2460 (ex-MET 103). The motorman is just releasing the handbrake as he proceeds towards Acton on this March day in 1935. (National Tramway Museum/H.Nicol)

HENDON DEPOT

12. Car 2377 is an ex-LUT vehicle of type U which was transferred by LT to replace some of the older ex-MET open toppers. The top deck cover of this tram has a distinctly home made look about it, and at this late stage in its career, a passenger on 2377 would have noticed a certain amount of "body movement" as the car picked up speed. In July 1936 this vehicle was scrapped. (D.Jones Coll.)

13. In the golden age of Hendon Depot a representative of MET type A waits to enter service. Some of the top deck seats have covers on them to keep out the wet weather. The original MET livery was vermilion (bright signal red) and ivory. The lettering COUNTY COUNCIL OF MIDDLESEX was in gold. Hendon Depot also housed an efficient tramcar repair facilty and the staff were kept busy maintaining and improving the fleet.   (R.J.Harley Coll.)

14. In June 1934, almost a year after the formation of London Transport, car 2463 is working a shuttle service for people attending Hendon Air Show. Extra trams would be drafted in to cater for the crowds eager to see those magnificent men (and women) in their flying machines. In the early 1930s air travel was only for the select few. Passengers are being allowed to board on the depot approach road, so that the special cars do not hold up regular service trams on the main road. (NTM/D.W.K.Jones)

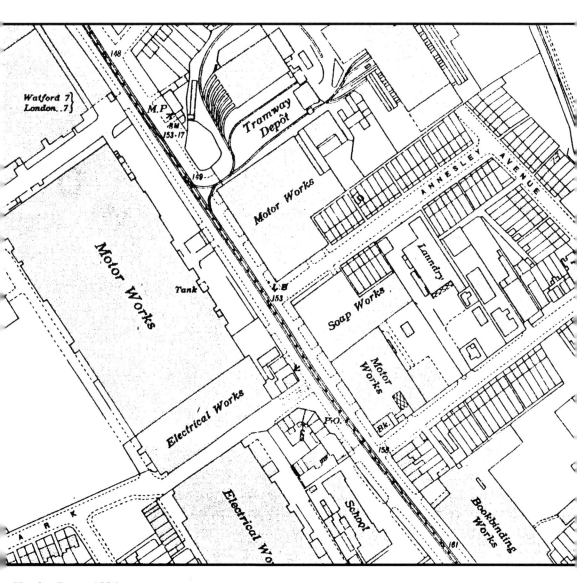

Hendon Depot 1936

15. Also in June 1934, MET car 6 halts for the photographer. We can note the splendid condition of this car (it was built in 1904) which has yet to be renumbered and repainted in full LT colours. As car 2498 it lasted until September 1935. (NTM/D.W.K.Jones)

———————►

16. Whilst the Air Show is in full flight, the earthbound transportation contingent is parked waiting for the evening rush home. On the left is car 161 (type C/2) and in the middle is former MET type B car 64. On the righthand side of the picture, on depot road 3, is former LUT car 267. This latter vehicle had an interesting history, as it worked all three company owned tramways in London. It was constructed in 1902 for the London United system, it received a top cover in 1910-11, and was later transferred in 1931 to work on routes operating from Sutton Depot of the SMET (South Metropolitan Electric Tramways). As can be seen here, its final resting place was in the western area of the MET. (NTM/D.W.K.Jones)

———————►

17. Hendon Depot was the site of an early trolleybus trial. On 25th September 1909 this 22-seater was taken for a spin around the yard. In reality this trolleybus never operated from Hendon to Golders Green Station, and soon afterwards the whole project quietly fizzled out. (D.Jones Coll.)

THE BURROUGHS HENDON GOLDERS GREEN STATION

METROPOLITAN ELECTRIC TRAMWAYS L^{TD}

THE RAILLESS ELECTRIC TRACTION C^o L^{TD}

18. The speed restriction notice on the wall behind car 2436 seems hardly appropriate as this courtege of tramcars has halted in anticipation of another rush of passengers. The motorman is in reflective mood as he examines his summer cap. (NTM/D.W.K.Jones)

30 **HARROW RD., (Scrubs Lane) — W. CROYDON**
Via Wormwood Scrubs, Wood Lane, Shepherds Bush, Hammersmith, Fulham Palace Rd., Putney, Wandsworth, Garratt Lane, Tooting, Mitcham Common, Croydon Rd., Mitcham Rd., Tamworth Road
Service Interval, 5—6 mins.   Journey time, 81 mins.
Principal fares : Harrow Rd.—Hammersmith Bdy. 3d. Hammersmith Bdy.—Putney High St. 2d., Putney High St. —Tooting Bdy. 3d., Tooting Bdy.—Mitcham Fair Grn. 2d., Mitcham Fair Grn.—W. Croydon 3d.

* to Mitcham (Fair Green).
† Change at Wandsworth, High Street.

Scrubs Lane to West Croydon	5 24	5 40	10†58	5 25	5 41	11† 6	7 58 11
Scrubs Lane to Mitcham (Fair Green)........	5 24	5 40	11 12	5 25	5 41	11 21	7 37 11
Scrubs Lane to York Road.................	4 37	5 25	11 41	4 37	5 25	11 41	7 37 11
Scrubs Lane to Hammersmith	4 37	5 25	12 31	4 37	5 25	2 1	7 37 12
West Croydon to Harrow Rd. (Scrubs Lane)..	4 44	5 17	11 10	4 44	5 17	11 30	8 37 11
West Croydon to Hammersmith...........	4 44	5 17	11 32	4 44	5 17	11 30	8 37 12
York Road to Harrow Rd. (Scrubs Lane)....	5 14	5 22	11 54	5 14	5 22	12 15	7 59 11
York Road to Hammersmith.................	5 14	5 22	12 57	5 14	5 22	12 52	7 59 12
York Road to Mitcham (Fair Green)..........	5 19	5 35	11 48	5 19	5 35	11 58	7 11 12
Mitcham (Fair Green) to Harrow Rd. (S. Lane)	5 3	5 36	11 29	5 3	5 36	11 50	7 36 11
Mitcham (Fair Green) to Hammersmith........	5 3	5 36	12 17	5 3	5 36	12 24	7 36 12
Hammersmith to Harrow Rd (Scrubs Lane)	4 20	5 6	12 13	4 20	5 8	1 44	7 20 12
Hammersmith to Tooting Junction..........	4 22	4 40	11 58	4 25	4 41	11 52	6 *53 12
Tooting Broadway to West Croydon........	5 35	5 50	11 51	5 35	5 51	12 1	8 27 11

WEST HENDON TO CRICKLEWOOD

19. Car 172 of type D makes its way along The Broadway, West Hendon. These vehicles, which conformed to a classic British, four wheel, open top design, were used in the Willesden/Edgware Road routes from the earliest years of operation. Note Batey's ginger beer carts about to start delivery runs. (B.J.Cross Coll.)

20. In contrast to the previous picture, we now encounter a larger, eight wheel car belonging to type C/1. Note the crossover in the foreground and the general lack of motorised traffic to challenge the tram's supremacy. (B.J.Cross Coll.)

21. Everyone is muffled up in this winter scene of a still rural area in the days before the Staples Corner interchange wrecked the landscape. Car 98 is depicted outside The Old Welsh Harp. As the shadows lengthen and dusk falls, then the faint circle of light from the gas lamps will be outdone by the electric headlamps and interior lights of passing tramcars.   (B.J.Cross Coll.)

22.   House building soon followed the inauguration of electric tramways, however, as we notice here, some open spaces were preserved. The array of hats on the top deck of car 105 would seem to indicate that a number of ladies have taken the opportunity of an outing to the shops.
(B.J.Cross Coll.)

23. We reach Cricklewood Broadway in company with car 200. We are looking north-west and can observe tracks and wires leading off to the right into Cricklewood Lane. (B.J.Cross Coll.)

5

NOTE: For all-night services see pages 192-193.

WHETSTONE (Totteridge L.)—CRICKLEWOOD
Via Church End, Temple Fortune, Golders Grn., ChildsHill.
Service interval. Cricklewood—Whetstone 6-8 mins.
Golders Grn.—Tally Ho Cnr. 2-8 mins
Curtailed at N. Finchley (Tally Ho Corner) Weekday
slack hours, and Sunday a.m. Journey time. Cricklewood—
Tally Ho Cnr. 24 mins.—Whetstone 30 mins.
Through fare 5d.

	MON. to FRI.		SATURDAY		SUNDAY	
	First	Last	First	Last	First	Last
Tally Ho Corner to Golders Green	5 0	5 7	11 52	5 0	5 7	12 3	1030	1151	......
Tally Ho Corner to Cricklewood	5 0	5 7	11 52	5 0	5 7	12 3	1030	1151	......
Golders Green to Tally Ho Corner	6 44	6 50	12 28	6 50	6 58	12 40	11 2	1223	......
Cricklewood to Tally Ho Corner	6 35	6 41	12 19	6 41	6 49	12 32	1054	1215	......
Cricklewood to Whetstone morning	6 35	6 41	8 45	6 41	7 10	8 46	......	......	......
" " afternoon	3 57	4 57	0	11 1	11 9	9 32	1 46	1019	......
Whetstone to Cricklewood morning	6 53	7 0	9 15	6 53	6 59	9 7	......	......	......
" " afternoon	4 29	4 36	7 31	1130	1140	10 3	2 20	1053	......

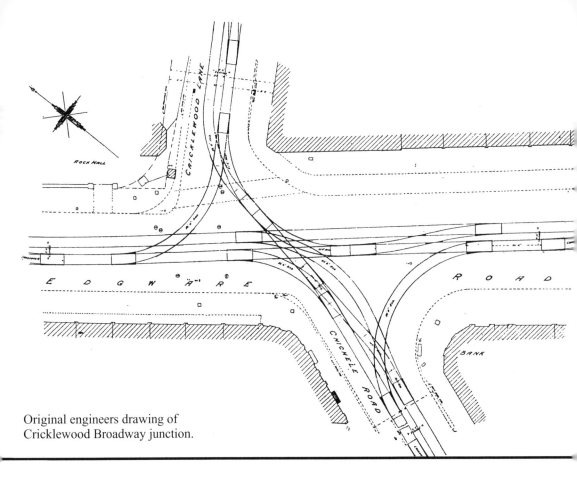

Original engineers drawing of
Cricklewood Broadway junction.

60 | **N. FINCHLEY — PADDINGTON (Edgware Rd.)**
Via Church End, Temple Fortune, Golders Green, Childs Hill, Cricklewood, Willesden, Harlesden, Harrow Rd. Service interval 6–8 mins. Journey time, 64 mins. Principal fares. N. Finchley—Golders Green 3d, Golders Green—Willesden Green Stn. 2d., Willesden Green Stn.—Paddington 6d.

Tally Ho Corner to Cricklewood	4	48	5	11	1220	4	48	5	11	1220	8 16 11 51 ......
Tally Ho Corner to Harlesden (Jubilee Clock)	4	48	5	11	1220	4	48	5	11	1220	8 16 11 45 ......
Tally Ho Corner to Paddington	4	48	5	11	11 0	4	48	5	11	1118	8 16 11 3 ......
Paddington to Tally Ho Corner	5	3	5	25	1212	5	3	5	25	1215	9 0 11 45 ......
Cricklewood to Tally Ho Corner	5	9	5	17	1255	5	5	5	17	1255	8 8 12 23 ......
Harlesden (Jubilee Clock) to Tally Ho Corner	4	51	4	59	1232	4	51	4	59	1235	7 50 12 5 ......

←

24. The well known steel trackwork specialists, Hadfield's of Sheffield, have supplied the junction layout at Cricklewood Broadway. Usually such intricate pieces were assembled in the maker's yard before being dismantled for shipment to the customer. All seems to be well here, and the standard gauge (1435mm) tracks have been laid with precision and skill. It is worth recalling that nearly all of this work was performed by labourers using only hand tools. (Middlesex C.C.)

25. We view this scene from a vantage point at the end of Chichele Road. The date is 26th April 1936 and we observe an Acton bound tram about to swing across the road towards us. An astute piece of footwork has enabled the PC on point duty to retain his dignity, whilst at the same time allowing the big red and cream monster free passage through the junction. (NTM/H.Nicol)

Cricklewood 1936

26. Dr.Hugh Nicol, the photographer, has repositioned himself on the other side of the Broadway. We now look from Cricklewood Lane into Chichele Road, following the line of tram route 60 which crossed here on its journey from North Finchley to Paddington. The curve to the right of the picture was used for depot workings to Hendon.   (NTM/H.Nicol)

27. Car 226 of type G is pictured in original open top condition. It is about to depart from Cricklewood Lane on its return journey to Finchley.   (B.J.Cross Coll.)

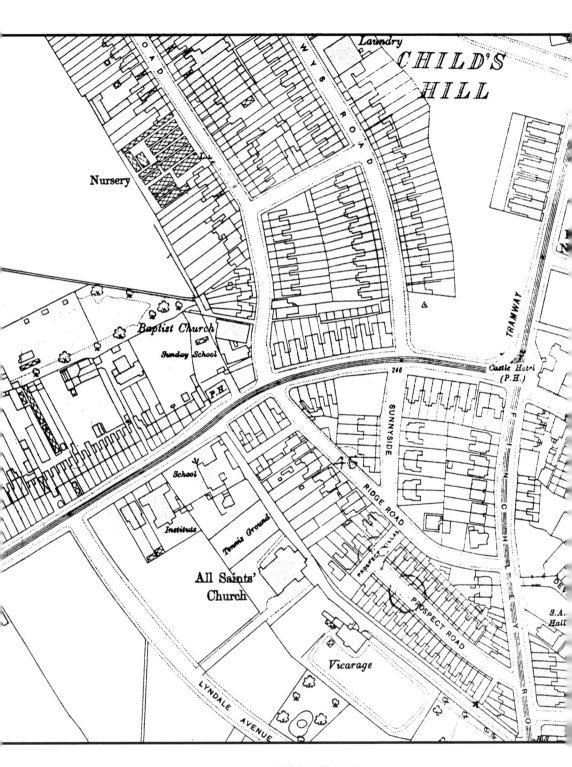

Childs Hill 1915

28. This view is included for its rarity value. It shows two type G cars passing at the junction of Cricklewood Lane and Finchley Road. Tracks lead off to the right behind cars 222 and 228; this formed part of the Childs Hill spur. This section of the MET was only employed in the early years to reverse cars and was soon thereafter abandoned.   (B.J.Cross Coll.)

29. The first tram terminus at Cricklewood suffered the same fate as its near neighbour at Childs Hill. The rails ended at the county boundary by Ash Grove. After 1915 the section of track illustrated here fell into disuse and the lines were later lifted.   (B.J.Cross Coll.)

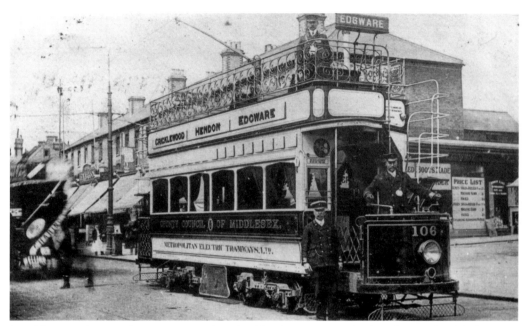

30. The smartly turned out crew members in this view attest to the fact that a job with the MET conferred a certain status. Car 106 also possesses a distinctive elegance. One can note the wire lifeguard below the collision fender. These lifeguards proved less than satisfactory in service; they bent out of shape and were prone to rust. The traditional wooden slat version soon replaced them. (B.J.Cross Coll.)

31. Our intention is to leave Cricklewood Broadway and take the tram along Chichele Road. Unfortunately we have just missed car 108, but as compensation we observe car 47 which is slowing for a compulsory stop. Note the use of the traction standard on the left as a convenient site for a sign directing the general public to the Metropolitan Railway station at Willesden Green, where the main line had been electrified in 1905. (B.J.Cross Coll.)

32. A stately colonnade of London plane trees masks the stop in Chichele Road opposite the post box on the corner of Rockhall Road. The architecture in this street looks so solid and reliable, an impression which is echoed by the oncoming car 274.   (J.B.Gent Coll.)

33. Cars 82 and 172 pass near the corner of Anson Road. The driver of the latter tram has a full canopy to offer some protection against the elements, but the crew of car 82 are fated to spend most of their time living an outdoor life to the full!   (R.J.Harley Coll.)

34. St.Gabriel's Church, Cricklewood probably would not win many plaudits for its design, but on this occasion the bright red and cream tramcar passing by has livened up the scene somewhat. Car 106 spent its entire life in MET colours and was scrapped before 1933 when the MET was incorporated into London Transport. (B.J.Cross Coll.)

→

35. Walm Lane is the setting for this picture of car 174. The route from Cricklewood to Willesden and beyond was beset by a number of curves which, it was thought, would be unsuitable for bogie cars, hence the use of the four wheel type D trams in this area. In practice this fear proved unfounded, and larger capacity vehicles soon appeared on this stretch of line. (Lens of Sutton)

→

36. Car 172 reappears, this time on Walm Lane and in pristine condition. The destination blind showing SPECIAL CAR lends weight to the argument that this vehicle had been newly overhauled and was on a test run when caught by the photographer's lens. Competition is apparent in the shape of a solid tyred, petrol engine bus on route 46. (J.B.Gent Coll.)

WILLESDEN TO HARLESDEN

37. The 1906 tram terminus at Willesden is depicted here. After the opening of the line from Cricklewood, cars reversed on the crossover situated on the bridge over the railway. At Christmas 1907 the service was extended to Craven Park, after local residents had expressed concern at the delay in providing them with modern public transport. (B.J.Cross Coll.)

38. Outside the White Horse, Church Road, car 88 halts at an ALL CARS STOP HERE sign. Note the heavier wires of the section feed which delivered 550 volts DC to the overhead. The white bands on the supporting traction standards reminded motormen to shut off power and coast under the section break. Application of power at this location could cause damaging electrical arcing and a risk of several blown fuses! (J.B.Gent Coll.)

39. In Church Road there were very few parking problems in the years before the First World War. Car 175 glides along past the many small shops so typical of the era. (D.Jones Coll.)

40. We arrive at Craven Park, at the junction with the lines leading to Stonebridge and Harlesden. Two MET D type cars occupy centre stage; the three firms of Liptons, Van Houten and Epps were prolific advertisers on London's tramways. Indeed, for many years cocoa was the staple, non-alcoholic drink of many poorer inhabitants of the capital. Only Liptons seem to have stood the test of time. (B.J.Cross Coll.)

41. Continuing our beverage theme, we note that car 22 sports the green and white LIPTON'S TEA advertisement; above is a blue and white notice which proclaims EMPIRE EXHIBITION CAR. This service was well patronised in 1924/25 when all roads led to Wembley. On the front platform the motorman turns his head to check on traffic coming from his left. The extended handrails on the top deck were installed to minimise the danger to passengers from a collapsed trolley spring. (F.Merton Atkins)

←

42. Crew changes at Craven Park junction might involve a short wait in the shelter to the right of car 125. The legend over the entrance reads FOR TRAM EMPLOYEES ONLY. (R.J.Harley Coll.)

←

43. Those who think that drought notices issued by the water boards are a modern affair, might like to read what is pasted on car 63! USE LESS WATER were the watchwords in this mid 1930s view. Aside from this stark warning, life goes on pretty much in the normal way - Fred Perry is writing his tennis column for the Evening News, and the patient conductor on the top deck is wondering how many more attempts his driver will need to get the trolley back on the wire. (NTM/D.W.K.Jones)

44. At Craven Park we meet an old stager in the shape of car 2405, yet another refugee from the LUT fleet. These vehicles were notoriously draught ridden and this defect was enhanced by the fact that the two centre windows on the top deck were unglazed. It is not surprising that on their home patch these cars were known as "influenza trams". It has also been alleged that LT deliberately kept these veterans in service to soften up public opinion in favour of the new, sleek, comfortable trolleybuses. Whatever the truth of this assertion, car 2405 soldiered on until scrapped in September 1936. (NTM/D.W.K.Jones)

45. The constable standing outside the police station takes note of car 92. As we shall see, this particular tram figures prominently in our narrative. Here it is pictured at the corner of St.Alban's Road. (B.J.Cross Coll.)

46. As predicted, car 92 shows up again in Craven Park Road. No doubt, the motorman has calculated that he can just pass the stationary horse and cart without tipping the whole show over!
(B.J.Cross Coll.)

47. It is a quarter past twelve on a bright day in 1907. Car 84 passes the corner of Manor Park Road, where the wine and spirit merchant has such an arresting name - fortunately in those days most Londoners were quite law abiding. (B.J.Cross Coll.)

48. We travel via High Street, Harlesden to arrive at the well known Jubilee Clock, which was commisioned in 1897 for the Diamond Jubilee of Queen Victoria. Car 88, on its way to Stonebridge Park, will shortly pass car 90 coming in the opposite direction. This postcard view is franked 10th July 1906.   (J.B.Gent Coll.)

49. There is evidence in this scene that the single curve from Station Road to the High Street was constructed after the initial layout was inaugurated. Passenger levels on car 100 seem healthy, in contrast to the forlorn situation of the horse bus parked opposite. (J.B.Gent Coll.)

50. We espy another tramcar, and we are not disappointed, for it is none other than our old favourite, car 92. Did the postcard publishers have a contract with the MET to extoll the virtues of this particular member of the fleet? We shall never know, but a more likely explanation is that car 92 was used exclusively on proving runs before the general commencement of public service. (B.J.Cross Coll.)

51. Forward in years to March 1925, and motor traffic is beginning to make an impact. Route numbers were first used on the MET in 1913, and here we observe a tram working route 62T. The letter T was an afterthought to avoid confusion with the bus services operated by the London General. This was rather odd, as most locals could easily tell the difference between a tram and a bus. (B.J.Cross Coll.)

←

52. The double track curves on the south-west side of the clock tower were installed in 1927. Car 86 received a top cover in 1929, and this helps date the photograph. Note that you could buy a made-to-measure suit for forty-two shillings (£2.10). (B.J.Cross Coll.)

←

53. Car 2395 approaches from Station Road and is about to turn left on the next stage of its journey to Canons Park. This tram was formerly LUT car 292; it was built in 1902, and received a top cover in 1911. In 1927 this car was partially modernised, thereby gaining more powerful motors and improved magnetic track brakes. Car 2395, of type U, was scrapped in July 1936. (D.Jones Coll.)

54. The sunblinds are down at the butcher's shop on the corner of Wendover Road. A warm summer's day is in prospect as car 196 wends its way in the distance. Its destination is Lock Bridge, the terminus reached by electric cars in December 1906. (J.B.Gent Coll.)

55. The former horse tram terminus was situated outside the Royal Oak, at the corner of High Street and Park Parade. On the extreme left of the picture is Webster's Newsagents, which reappears in the next picture. On the right of this view a solitary horse car waits to begin its leisurely amble along Harrow Road to Lock Bridge. (J.B.Gent Coll.)

56. We remain outside Webster's for our last look at Harlesden High Street. The electric age has dawned and what better representative to demonstrate this new era of grace than our old friend, car 92. (B.J.Cross Coll.)

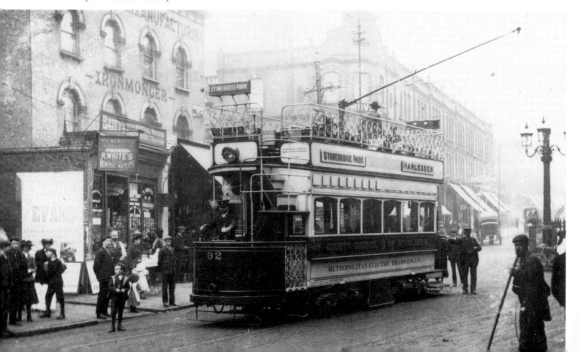

57. Car 60 is pictured at the top of Station Road after having passed under a section feed. Note the well maintained track and road surface, features typical of the efficient MET. However, all is not well and marks in the foreground betray a derailment at this location. Obviously a bogie car has recently come to grief on the Acton bound curve, and an internal enquiry will take place to ascertain the cause of this break in service.   (B.J.Cross Coll.)

58. The terrace houses on Station Road echo the sound of a descending tramcar, as it sweeps past Harlesden Parish Church.   (R.J.Harley Coll.)

59. At the bottom of the hill by Honeywood Road, the MET engineers could not quite squeeze in their customary double track, so interlaced rails became the order of the day. This feature is also know as gauntlet track. We observe all this on a very wet 4th September 1931. (NTM/H.Nicol)

60. The parked car on the left indicates a probable reason for interlaced track at this spot, but many other, narrower roads in London boasted double track. The reason may have something to do with the shopkeepers and other frontagers demanding their rights as to the minimum space between the kerb and the outer rail. Whatever the cause, at least the MET saved on points! (Lens of Sutton)

61. We near Willesden Junction Station and the motorman gives a friendly wave to Dr.Nicol. All fleets have to start somewhere, and as the car number suggests, this vehicle was the first on any tramspotters list. On the front canopy the advert for Bovril sets a new standard in puns. (NTM/H.Nicol)

62. Next tram along is car 90, but this time the
motorman looks a little more guarded about his
image being preserved for posterity. He may be
wondering why anyone should want to waste film
on such a mundane object as a tramcar. After all
there were thousands of them all over the country.
However, enthusiasts, local historians and all
lovers of London's past are in debt to the handful
of people who pursued the hobby throughout the
1920s and 1930s. Their work has left us an
accurate record of a bygone era. One final note
about car 90 is that it was fitted with a top cover
in 1928, and this view was taken very shortly
afterwards. (NTM/H.Nicol)

⟶

63. The date is 1st June 1929 and car 119 is
standing at Acton terminus. This remained the
end of the line for electric traction until 1936,
when the replacing trolleybuses were extended
round the corner over ex LUT tracks in the
direction of Hammersmith. (NTM/H.Nicol)

64. An earlier view of Acton terminus reveals car 80 which is conceivably working back to the depot at Hendon.   (C.Carter Coll.)

NOTE: For all-night services, see pages 192-193.

62 SUDBURY — PADDINGTON (Edgware Rd.) Via Wembley, Stonebridge Park, Craven Park, Harlesden, Kensal Green, Harrow Road. Service interval, 6-10 minutes. Journey time, Paddington—Stonebridge Pk. 27 mins.,— Sudbury 40 mins. Through fare 7d.		MON. to FRI.		SATURDAY		SUND	
		First	Last	First	Last	First	La
	Sudbury to Stonebridge Park	5 47	6 3	5 47	6 3	9 6	1210
	Sudbury to Paddington	5 47	6 3	5 47	6 3	9 6	1210
	Stonebridge Park to Paddington	4 10	4 26	4 10	4 26	8 32	1133
	Stonebridge Park to Sudbury	5 24	5 41	5 24	5 41	8 53	1156
	Wembley to Paddington	5 51	6 7	5 51	6 7	9 10	1124
	Paddington to Sudbury	4 57	5 15	4 57	5 15	9 5	1129
	Paddington to Wembley	4 57	5 15	4 57	5 15	9 5	1129
	Paddington to Stonebridge Park	4 40	4 57	4 40	4 57	9 5	12 2

SCRUBS LANE

65. The inclusion of an LCC car in a book dominated by the MET may seem to be out of place, but E/1 class car 987 is actually standing on LCC metals, a few yards inside the county boundary. The location was referred to as College Park and this view dates from 1908-10 before the connection with the MET tracks in Harrow Road was inserted. (D.Jones Coll.)

EDGWARE — PADDINGTON (Edgware Road). Via Colindale, Hendon, Cricklewood, Willesden, Craven Park, Harlesden, Harrow Road. Service Interval, Wkdy rush hrs only, 8 mins. Journey time, 62 mins. Through fare 10d.	Edgware to Paddington	morning	7	4	7 21	7 54	7	4	7 21	7 54	......	......	......
	,, ,, ,, ...	afternoon	3 22	3 28	6 26		11 14	11 22	2	0	......	......	......
	Paddington to Edgware............	morning	6 16	6 24	8	8	6 16	6 24	8	8	......	......	......
	,, ,, ...	afternoon	4 32	4 40	7 28		12 8	12 24	2	16	......	......	......

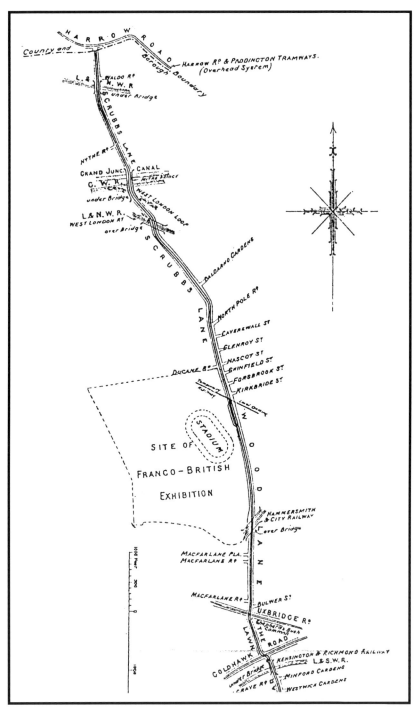

Original track layout of the Wood Lane/Scrubs Lane extension.

66. The Mitre Bridge over the Grand Junction Canal and Great Western Railway was (and still is) an interesting structure. Here car 997 pauses whilst LCC officials carry out clearance and deflection tests, before the official 30th May 1908 opening. (R.J.Harley Coll.)

67. During 1908 work continued frantically outside the Franco British Exhibition in Wood Lane. Tracks and wires are in position for the new LCC service, and the contractors are putting the finishing touches to the road surface. Futher along the road the LCC constructed a tramway siding and loading area for visitors to the exhibition; unfortunately this farsighted piece of transport planning was removed in 1911. (J.B.Gent Coll.)

HARROW ROAD TO PADDINGTON

68. Car 255 is caught by the camera in early days on the Harrow Road. It is one of a batch of ten H type cars which worked the route to Lock Bridge. This car in common with others of types D and H which were allocated to this route did not bear the familiar COUNTY COUNCIL OF MIDDLESEX on the waist panel. The lettering was superfluous, as this end of the line lay well and truly in London County Council territory. (V.Whitbread)

69. Sunlight catches newly delivered car 182, which like all its sisters in type D, was a sturdy looking tram capable of being put to work almost anywhere on the MET system. Indeed, many later migrated to the Wood Green area, and the subsequent fitting of plough gear enabled this type to work through services to central London. (B.J.Cross Coll.)

70. The motorman of car 155 seems to be concentrating on some goings on to the left of the picture. His tram belongs to type C; it was later given a top cover and reclassified type C/2. Renumbered 2487 by LT, it survived until August 1936. (B.J.Cross Coll.)

71. Paddington tramway terminus, like its GWR namesake, acted like a magnet for photographers, hence this view of car 38 which is the first of many. Note that the trolley pole has already been reversed and the tram is about to use the crossover to regain the correct side of the highway. (G.N.Southerden)

72. Car 2431 is in full LT livery as it waits to join the queue for the terminus.
(NTM/M.J.O'Connor)

73. From the look of things the inspector in the foreground has just told the joke about the General bus which tried to squeeze between two MET trams on the Harrow Road and ended up a motorcycle with a load of very tall, thin passengers! Perhaps they had to keep their spirits up, after all it was January 1931, and the open platforms and top deck of car 60 were not the most comfortable places to be when chill winds blew.
(NTM/H.Nicol)

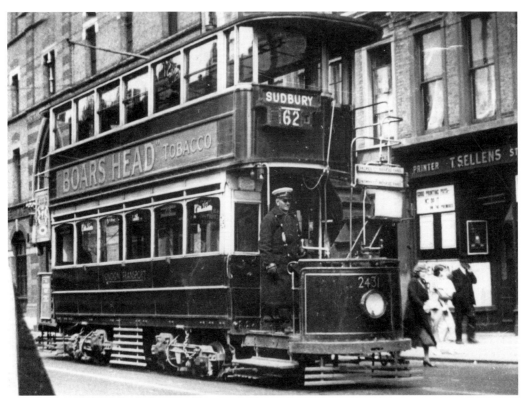

←——————

74. The weather has improved since the last view and the top deck of car 91 is once more a pleasant place to observe the hustle and bustle of a great metropolis. Road works seem to have closed off the last few yards of track before the junction with Edgware Road.   (G.N.Southerden)

←——————

75. This is a scene taken looking north towards an unidentified MET car. Between the trucks can be noted the wooden "dog gate" which was supposed to prevent inquisitive canines from taking an enforced tram ride when the car started up again. Small dogs, accompanied by their owners, were allowed on the top deck at the discretion of the conductor, but it has to be said that the real animal star of the transport world was the depot cat, which has an assured place in tramway folklore. On the side of the car the blue and white NEWS OF THE WORLD banner also appeared on many LCC trams.
(E.G.P.Masterman)

76.   MET car 81 is seen in its LT identity as car 2418. Inspite of its impending withdrawal, this tram is still maintained in excellent condition. (G.N.Southerden)

77. Car 2487, ex MET car 155, loads at Paddington. The motorman peers round to check that the lower saloon is filling up; he may be anxious to depart, as only minimal "stand" time was allocated to this busy terminus. The advert on the dash encompasses two icons of British heroism: Winston Churchill has written a newspaper article on Lawrence of Arabia. (G.N.Southerden)

78. Paddington terminus was situated close to the West End, but any thoughts of linking it with the LCC tramways at Victoria were quashed by wealthy residents and landowners who objected to tramcars. Thus the through traffic was left to the buses and underground railways. Ironically not even the trolleybuses reached this far, and they were banished to a turning circle at Paddington Green. (B.J.Cross Coll.)

79. A few moments after the previous picture, and car 2436 has now usurped car 2494's slot for departure. The service interval on route 62 was a car every six to ten minutes, so late running left little margin to make up lost time. (B.J.Cross Coll.)

STONEBRIDGE PARK
DEPOT TO SUDBURY

80. "Odd man out" car 77 was given the full treatment at Hendon Depot and emerged in 1929 with updated body styling. Here it is seen as LT car 2412. The route number stencil box seems to be jammed up to such an extent that travellers to Wembley could be forgiven for thinking that they would be charged four dollars for the experience. (D.Jones Coll.)

81. Hill Side, Stonebridge and car 125 rolls along with a full load. Note the man with the pickaxe who is effecting some urgent road repairs. (B.J.Cross Coll.)

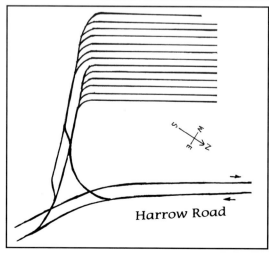

Plan of Stonebridge Park Depot.

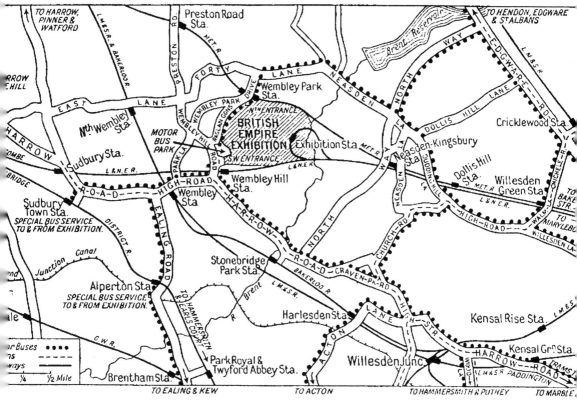

82. Stonebridge Park Depot is pictured in 1906. On display are cars 189 and 155; on road one we meet up again with car 92. On the left of the picture is a single horse car. It has been suggested that this tram was kept so that the MET could maintain an occasional service on the Chippenham Road branch to keep it open legally in case of eventual electrification. (B.J.Cross Coll.)

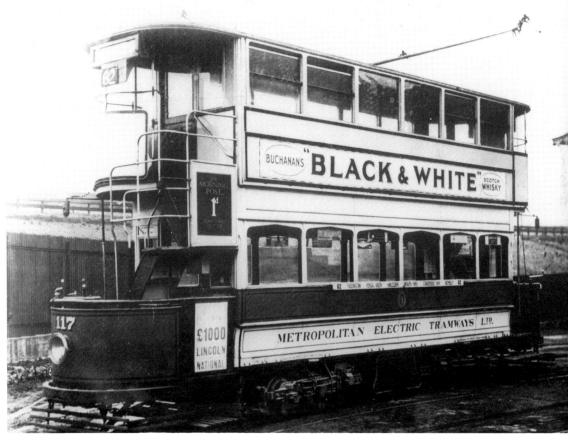

84. The depot forecourt was a natural spot to photograph newly overhauled cars. Car 117 was later renumbered 2463 by London Transport. In the background is the embankment of the former LNWR line to Watford which was electrified in 1917. (D.Jones Coll.)

83. A formal photograph has obviously been required before car 35 goes out on the Empire Exhibition special service. The depot was opened on 10th October 1906 and originally supplied twenty trams. The full capacity was 48 trams on twelve tracks which were under cover. (B.J.Cross Coll.)

85. Car 9 stands waiting for its crew. Note the livery details; from 1929 the word METROPOLITAN appeared in gold letters on the waist panel. The Middlesex coat of arms is in the centre of the rocker panel. The Metropolitan Stage Carriage licence plate, in this case no.8976, was affixed to one end of the car. The white triangle bearing the words EIGHT WHEEL BRAKES was a warning device for motorists not to come too close. (D.Jones Coll.)

86. The next three views form a set published to commemorate the arrival of the first electric trams at the new Stonebridge Park terminus. Initially the rails ended at the Iron Bridge, and service commenced on 10th October 1906 after a delay of some weeks whilst the Metropolitan Water Board carried out mains work. As we have come to expect, car 92 gets into the act very quickly! (R.J.Harley Coll.)

87. Another candidate for the photographer's lens is car 84. Note the poses struck by some of the participants, and was that a symbolic touch, placing the chap with the bike nextdoor to the new wonder of modern electrical science? (B.J.Cross Coll.)

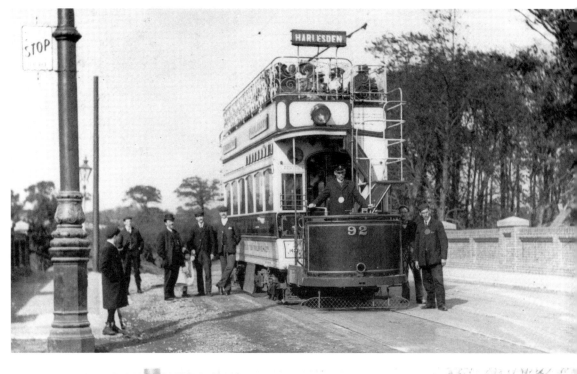

88. Our final view from this trio is of car 151. In this scene the audience seems to have lost interest and gone home. However, the work of the MET goes on, and in the background rails have been stacked for the new route to Wembley which will pass through open countryside. (B.J.Cross Coll.)

89. Wembley was soon built up after the trams arrived in April 1908. Here at The Green a 93 bus moves on to the main road, while to the left a couple of MET trams on route 62 are about to pass. In theory this growing suburb was well served by public transport, but after the opening of Wembley Stadium, it was all hands to the pumps on football match days. In their time the trams must have moved millions of spectators to cup finals and other sporting occasions. (B.J.Cross Coll.)

90. Street accidents always provide good copy for local newspapers and this contretemps in Wembley High Road was no exception. It certainly was the battle of the heavyweights - tram v. traction engine. (R.J.Harley Coll.)

TRAMCAR IN COLLISION.—A tramcar and a traction engine which wer
Wembley High-road yesterday. A passenger in the car complained of sho
medical aid. Both tracks were obstructed for some time.

←———————

91. As has been mentioned, some parts of the Wembley route were still very rural when the trams were introduced. This was an advantage for motormen who wished to speed on a section with practically no competing traffic. Note that even on undeveloped roads the progressive MET always laid double track. The practice of some London municipal systems which installed single track and loops was frowned upon by the MET. (B.J.Cross Coll.)

93. The rather grandly named, Universe House, provides the backdrop for this view of car 4. From a style point of view, inspite of its faults, car 4 has the edge over the slab like conformity of the building opposite. From 23rd August 1936 the replacing trolleybuses on route 662 used a turning circle based on a new roundabout. The trams, being double ended, did not need all these major road works, and as can be seen here, reversing was a very simple job. (NTM/M.J.O'Connor)

←———————

92. We now arrive at Sudbury terminus and we observe car 161 being made ready for the return to Paddington. These cars always look rather ill proportioned, an effect created by the cream painted sheet metal work round the top deck balcony. One wonders why the MET did not go the whole hog and completely enclose the top deck. (NTM/H.Nicol)

94. Car 293 is advertising the MET's associated electrical supply company.
Boards below the lower deck windows encourage passengers to change at
Westbourne Park Station, presumably on to the trains of the Hammersmith
and City line. This vehicle has no plough gear, but in 1919-20 all former
Stonebridge cars of type H were transferred to other depots, and then fitted
with ploughs so that they could work joint services with the LCC.
(B.J.Cross Coll.)

95. In our final look at Sudbury we catch sight of car 266 as it waits at the terminus. Above it is a triangle of wires which forms the trolley reverser. Although these ingenious devices were used by several provincial tramways, they never caught on in London. Crew members were just so used to swinging the pole by hand.   (B.J.Cross Coll.)

56

CANONS PARK — HENDON — ACTON
Via Edgware, Burnt Oak, Colindale, Hendon, Dollis Hill
Cricklewood, Willesden Green, Willesden Craven Park
Harlesden, Willesden Junction, North Acton.
Service interval, Acton—Willesden Green Stn. 8 mins.
Willesden Green Stn.—Edgware 4-8 mins. Edgware—
Canons Park 8 mins. Journey time, 62 minutes.
Principal fares, Acton—Cricklewood 4d, Cricklewood—
Canons Park 5d.
* Change at Cricklewood.
‡ from Stonebridge Park. 7 mins earlier. E to Edgware.

Route			
Canons Park to Acton	7 30 7 38 10 59	7 30 7 38 11 3	12 7 10 42
Canons Park to Harlesden (Jubilee Clock)	7 30 7 38 10 59	7 30 7 38 11*11	12 7 10 42
Edgware to Acton	4 48 5 9 11 3	4 48 5 9 11 7	8 31 10 46
Edgware to Harlesden (Jubilee Clock)	4 48 5 9 12*31	4 48 5 9 12*43	8 31 11*56
Hendon to Acton	4 42 4 56 11 11	4 42 4 56 11 15	8 13 10 53
Hendon to Harlesden (Jubilee Clock)	4 42 4 56 12*47	4 42 4 56 12*51	8 13 12*30
Acton to Canons Park	6 27 6 35 9 56	6 27 6 35 10* 6	11 7 9 39
Acton to Edgware	5 26 5 42 11 32	5 26 5 42 11 43	9 0 10 59
Acton to Hendon	5 26 5 42 12 0	5 26 5 42 12 3	9 0 11 42
Acton to Harlesden (Jubilee Clock)	5 26 5 42 12 0	5 26 5 42 12 3	9 0 11 42
Harlesden (Jubilee Clock) to Canons Park	6 41 6 49 10 10	6 41 6 49 10*23	11 19 9 53
Harlesden (Jubilee Clock) to Edgware	4 6 4 27 11 44	4 6 4 27 11 58	7*50 11 13
Harlesden (Jubilee Clock) to Hendon	4 6 4 27 12*45	4 6 4 27 12*47	7*50 12*28
Harlesden (Jubilee Clock) to Acton	5‡10 5 20 11 46	5‡10 5 20 11 48	8 46 11 26
Cricklewood to Hendon	4E24 4E45 1 4	4E24 4E45 1 9	8 9 12 47

ROLLING STOCK

MET type D cars 166-190. These trams were built by Brush in 1906. They rode on 6ft./1829mm wheelbase, four wheel trucks of the Brush AA type. After the first World War they were modified to carry plough gear and the trucks were subsequently lengthened by 17ins/432mm. Seating was for 22 in the lower saloon and for 32 on the top deck. In 1931 most of this type went for scrap.

96. Car 191 was classified type D/1 and as is apparent, possessed a three window lower deck. This tram was built by Brush in 1903 as a sample car; it was sold to the MET in July 1904. This view was taken before 1920-21 when car 191 was altered to conform with the rest of type D. (D.Jones Coll.)

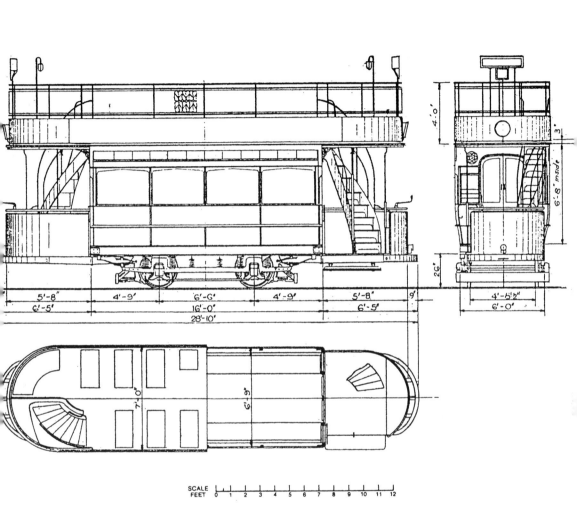

SCALE FEET | 0 1 2 3 4 5 6 7 8 9 10 11 12

BODY - Brush El Eng Co Ltd.	TRUCK - Brush 'A' Type.	EQUIPMENT - 2 GE Motors	METROPOLITAN ELECTRIC TWY.
Seating 22 + 31 = 53	Wheels 31¾" diameter. Axles Journals.	Controllers B.T.H.	4 WHEEL OPEN TOP TRAM

TYPE: 'D'

SCALE: 4 mm = 1 Foot

DRAWING No. TC 96

97. A standard type D car is pictured in original condition. Note the headlamp positioned on the top deck canopy. (W.Gratwicke)

MET type UCC cars 319, 321-329 and 332-375. These revolutionary new vehicles were delivered in 1930/31. They were always known as Felthams because the Union Construction Company's works was situated in Victoria Road, Feltham. They were steel framed cars with lightweight metal panels, although thicker material was used to reinforce the dashes and driver's cabs. They rode on maximum traction trucks, and each truck had a 70hp motor. Each car was fitted with two trolley poles, and plough gear was installed as standard.

98. The Felthams were most enthusiast's favourites and it has been claimed
that London has yet to see a more luxurious public transport vehicle. Shortly
after delivery, car 348 is seen working over LCC conduit tracks. Note the
fine lines of the car and the elevated driving position which gave the motorman
a comfortable view of the road ahead.   (NTM/M.J.O'Connor)

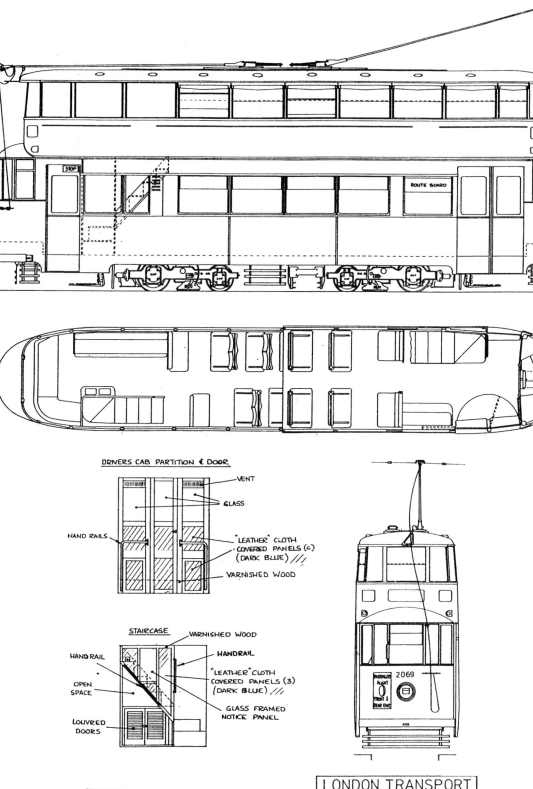

STOP

ROUTE BOARD

DRIVERS CAB PARTITION & DOOR

VENT

GLASS

HAND RAILS

"LEATHER" CLOTH
COVERED PANELS (6)
(DARK BLUE) ///

VARNISHED WOOD

STAIRCASE

VARNISHED WOOD

HANDRAIL

HANDRAIL

"LEATHER" CLOTH
COVERED PANELS (3)
(DARK BLUE) ///

OPEN
SPACE

GLASS FRAMED
NOTICE PANEL

LOUVRED
DOORS

PASSENGERS
ALIGHT
FRONT &
REAR END

2069

DRAWN BY TERRY RUSSELL "CHACESIDE"
ST. LEONARDS PARK HORSHAM W. SUSSEX.
INTERIOR DETAIL KINDLY SUPPLIED
BY ROBERT WATKINS.

LONDON TRANSPORT
D/DECK TRAMCAR

TYPE: Ex M.E.T. & L.U.T.
UCC "FELTHAM"

SCALE:
4 mm = 1 Foot

DRAWING No. TC 5

99. Unfortunately the era of the London tramcar was over by the time the policy makers at 55, Broadway (London Transport HQ) got their way. Here car 2104, ex MET car 360, ekes out its last days before transfer south of the river to Telford Avenue Depot. As befits a tram equipped with separate entrances and exits, the notice on the front gives the relevant information to passengers and to following motorists who have to pay particular attention when the tram is loading at stops. (R.J.Harley Coll.)

100. A close up of the air operated front door reveals the red and white STOP warning sign. We can note also the driver's cabin which placed him for the first time away from the stairs leading to the upper saloon. This photo was taken in October 1947 and is of car 2136 which was a former London United vehicle. (G.F.Ashwell)

101. On the post war system, the ride from Croydon to Purley gave motormen the opportunity to put the Felthams through their paces. Here car 2120 accelerates past the photographer. (D.A.Thompson)

102. Sunshine floods the upper saloon of car 2105, ex MET car 361, on an August day in 1947. Comfortable seats are positioned in a light and airy environment, totally unlike the top deck of a traditional London tram with its matchboarding and wooden bulkhead doors. (A.J.Watkins)

103. The lower deck also looks inviting. This April 1947 view shows the interior of car 2096. To the left of the conductor is the straight staircase leading to the upper saloon. No smoking was allowed in the lower saloon. (G.F.Ashwell)

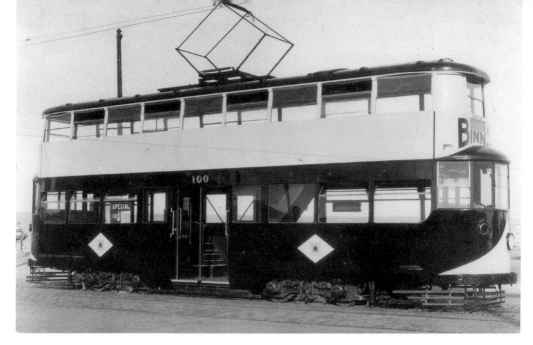

104. MET experimental Feltham car 331 was described in companion volume *Barnet and Finchley Tramways*. It was sold in 1937 to Sunderland where it is pictured as car 100. It is shown here to demonstrate the versatility of the Feltham design, and gives an indication as to what might have been, had London Transport not been so anti-tram. (R.J.Harley Coll.)

105. The Felthams were sold in 1949-51 to Leeds. They were repainted in a different red livery and each one received a bow collector in place of the twin trolleys. Leeds car 503 is ex LT car 2077, ex MET car 333. All of which illustrates the durability of these remarkable trams. (R.J.Harley Coll.)

OVERHEAD WIRING

Fears that a plethora of wires would make many thoroughfares unsightly proved groundless, and as the following photos show, some of the overhead layouts were very well designed. All London tramway operators adopted overhead wires but in central London the LCC used the conduit system of current collection and this has been fully described in **Embankment and Waterloo Tramways**. *An alternative to the trolley pole was the bow collector and this method gained in popularity in the 1930s. However, apart from two experiments by the MET and the LCC, the trolley pole remained until the end in July 1952. It is interesting to speculate what might have happened had either the LCC or MET switched to bow collectors. One wonders whether the trolleybus advocates would have been so vocal, bearing in mind the alleged difficulties of mixing trolleybuses and bow collector equipped trams. Certainly this was one of the arguments advanced in Glasgow for limiting the size of the trolleybus system. As it turned out during the pre-war conversion programme, the trams often used the trolleybus positive wire in the transition period.*

106. Centre poles, like these in use on the MET at Tottenham, are one of the most elegant methods of overhead suspension. We can admire the wrought iron work and craftmanship that goes into producing each traction standard. These fine specimens were not to last, however, because they were deemed an obstruction to the increasing numbers of motorists. (D.Jones Coll.)

107. The simple and effective span wire method of overhead suspension is shown at its neatest on the MET system. Green painted standards were planted in the pavement on opposite sides of the carriageway. The examples shown here will shortly be replaced by more substantial trolleybus standards, which will be required to support twice the amount of overhead. (D.Jones Coll.)

Catalogue drawings of overhead equipment

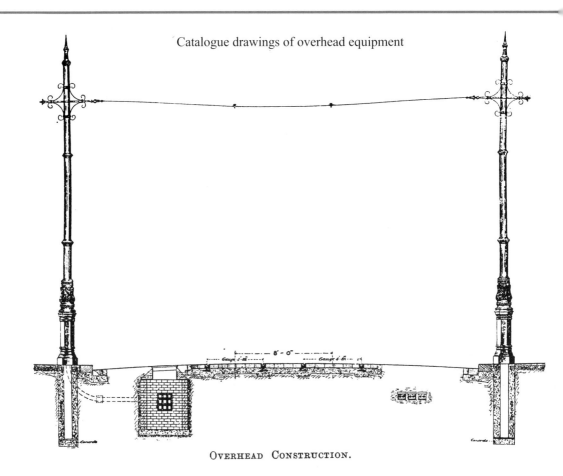

OVERHEAD CONSTRUCTION.

108. On curves a web like structure was employed to guide the trolley pole. This can clearly be seen above car 121. (D.Jones Coll.)

lower right

109. Sometimes bracket arms would be used to support the overhead wires. Bexley car 4 is depicted with its trolley mast, which was a metal column fixed to the top deck floor. This type was normal equipment on open top cars. (A.J.Watkins Coll.)

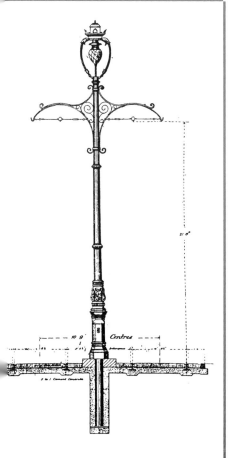

110. Tramway traction standards could carry street lights as here at Thornton Heath Pond in Croydon, or they could provide a suitable post for a variety of street, direction and traffic signs. Just above the bus in this view can be seen the thicker wires supplying a power feed to the running wires. Finally we can note a number of different shaped ears whose function was to clamp the running wires to the supporting span wires. (R.J.Harley Coll.)

111. Another useful overhead fitting was the skate which is directly above car 100. As the trolley head made contact with this apparatus, an electrical signal was sent to the nearby traffic lights, so that they would register the approach of the tramcar. (R.J.S.Wiseman)

112. In McLeod Road, Abbey Wood, there was dual working of trams and trolleybuses. Extended trolleybus spacer bars were used to cope with the triple overhead. Thus it was possible for a 36/38 tram to overtake a 698 trolleybus, and of course an impatient trolleybus driver could always try to nip through on the inside. (J.H.Meredith)

113. On occasions the tram went one way and the trolley pole went the other. This inevitably used to lead to a dewirement. The cause could be human error or a fault in the overhead frog (points). Hopefully here in Beresford Square, Woolwich, the conductor has spotted the trouble in time. (R.J.Harley Coll.)

114. The business end of the trolley pole is the swivel trolley head as illustrated at a display in the National Tramway Museum. The swivel head contains a grooved trolley wheel which maintains contact with the running wire. At the other end of the trolley pole a sprung pivot attached to the roof of the tram maintains the tension of the pole and allows free lateral and vertical movement. (R.J.Harley)

115. A tramway oddity in London was the double trolley route from Woolwich to Lee Green via Eltham. This lasted from 1910 to 1927. The full story is told in *Eltham and Woolwich Tramways*. Suffice to say here that this is a March 1927 picture of LCC car 1399. (NTM/H.Nicol)

116. A search was always on to find a current collector which might be less prone to dewirement. In 1927, MET cars 3 and 34 were fitted with bow collectors; this necessitated some allteration of the overhead in the Finchley area where the experiment took place. In the end the trials only lasted two years and the MET stuck with the tried and tested trolley pole. The LCC also conducted similar tests on the Grove Park route. (MET)

117. A fleet of service vehicles had to be on hand to maintain and repair the overhead. Here are three splendid specimens of overhead tower wagons poised for action outside the former SMET depot at Aurelia Road. (D.Jones Coll.)

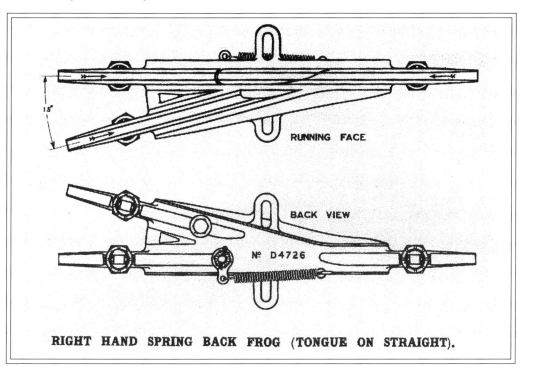

RIGHT HAND SPRING BACK FROG (TONGUE ON STRAIGHT).

FINALE

118. Car 2369 is already using the positive wire of the new trolleybus overhead. This indicates that the demise of the local tramways is imminent. On the right of the picture one of the new trolleybuses stands in Hendon Depot yard. (NTM/ M.J.O'Connor)

119. Trolleybus 223 is being employed to train crews at Hendon Depot. LT invested large sums in conversion work at both Hendon and Stonebridge Park. In the case of the latter it amounted to a complete rebuild of the depot and a replanning of the entrance road to the depot forecourt. (NTM/D.W.K.Jones)

120. The local trolleybuses now belong just as much to the past as do the MET tramcars. Things look deceptively permanent for this 662 trolleybus pictured at College Park, but in a few years all will be swept away in an unhealthy gale of diesel fumes. (C.Carter)

MP Middleton Press

Easebourne Lane, Midhurst, West Sussex. GU29 9AZ Tel: 01730 813169 Fax: 01730 812601

... WRITE OR PHONE FOR OUR LATEST LIST ...

BRANCH LINES
Branch Line to Allhallows
Branch Lines to Alton
Branch Lines around Ascot
Branch Line to Ashburton
Branch Lines around Bodmin
Branch Line to Bude
Branch Lines around Canterbury
Branch Line to Cheddar
Branch Lines to East Grinstead
Branch Lines to Effingham Junction
Branch Line to Fairford
Branch Line to Hawkhurst
Branch Line to Hayling
Branch Lines to Horsham
Branch Line to Ilfracombe
Branch Line to Kingswear
Branch Lines to Longmoor
Branch Line to Lyme Regis
Branch Line to Lynton
Branch Lines around Midhurst
Branch Line to Minehead
Branch Lines to Newport (IOW)
Branch Line to Padstow
Branch Lines around Plymouth
Branch Lines around Portmadoc 1923-46
Branch Lines around Porthmadog 1954-94
Branch Lines to Seaton & Sidmouth
Branch Line to Selsey
Branch Lines around Sheerness
Branch Line to Southwold
Branch Line to Swanage
Branch Line to Tenterden
Branch Lines to Torrington
Branch Lines to Tunbridge Wells
Branch Line to Upwell
Branch Lines around Wimborne
Branch Lines around Wisbech

SOUTH COAST RAILWAYS
Ashford to Dover
Brighton to Eastbourne
Chichester to Portsmouth
Dover to Ramsgate
Hastings to Ashford
Portsmouth to Southampton
Ryde to Ventnor
Worthing to Chichester

SOUTHERN MAIN LINES
Bromley South to Rochester
Charing Cross to Orpington
Crawley to Littlehampton
Dartford to Sittingbourne
East Croydon to Three Bridges
Epsom to Horsham
Exeter to Barnstaple
Exeter to Tavistock
Faversham to Dover
Haywards Heath to Seaford
London Bridge to East Croydon
Orpington to Tonbridge
Sittingbourne to Ramsgate
Swanley to Ashford
Tavistock to Plymouth
Victoria to East Croydon
Waterloo to Windsor

Waterloo to Woking
Woking to Portsmouth
Woking to Southampton
Yeovil to Exeter

COUNTRY RAILWAY ROUTES
Andover to Southampton
Bournemouth to Evercreech Jn.
Burnham to Evercreech Junction
Croydon to East Grinstead
Didcot to Winchester
Fareham to Salisbury
Frome to Bristol
Guildford to Redhill
Porthmadog to Blaenau
Reading to Basingstoke
Reading to Guildford
Redhill to Ashford
Salisbury to Westbury
Strood to Paddock Wood
Taunton to Barnstaple
Wenford Bridge to Fowey
Westbury to Bath
Woking to Alton
Yeovil to Dorchester

GREAT RAILWAY ERAS
Ashford from Steam to Eurostar
Clapham Junction 50 years of change
Festiniog in the Fifties
Festiniog in the Sixties
Isle of Wight Lines 50 years of change

LONDON SUBURBAN RAILWAYS
Caterham and Tattenham Corner
Clapham Jn. to Beckenham Jn.
Crystal Palace and Catford Loop
East London Line
Finsbury Park to Alexandra Palace
Holborn Viaduct to Lewisham
Kingston and Hounslow Loops
Lines around Wimbledon
London Bridge to Addiscombe
Mitcham Junction Lines
North London Line
South London Line
West Croydon to Epsom
West London Line
Willesden Junction to Richmond
Wimbledon to Epsom

STEAM PHOTOGRAPHERS
O.J.Morris's Southern Railways 1919-59

STEAMING THROUGH
Steaming through Cornwall
Steaming through East Sussex
Steaming through the Isle of Wight
Steaming through Kent
Steaming through West Hants
Steaming through West Sussex

TRAMWAY CLASSICS
Aldgate & Stepney Tramways
Barnet & Finchley Tramways
Bath Tramways
Bournemouth & Poole Tramways

Brighton's Tramways
Bristol's Tramways
Camberwell & W.Norwood Tramways
Clapham & Streatham Tramways
Dover's Tramways
East Ham & West Ham Tramways
Edgware and Willesden Tramways
Eltham & Woolwich Tramways
Embankment & Waterloo Tramways
Enfield & Wood Green Tramways
Exeter & Taunton Tramways
Gosport & Horndean Tramways
Greenwich & Dartford Tramways
Hampstead & Highgate Tramways
Hastings Tramways
Holborn & Finsbury Tramways
Ilford & Barking Tramways
Kingston & Wimbledon Tramways
Lewisham & Catford Tramways
Liverpool Tramways 1. Eastern Routes
Maidstone & Chatham Tramways
North Kent Tramways
Portsmouth's Tramways
Reading Tramways
Seaton & Eastbourne Tramways
Southampton Tramways
Southend-on-sea Tramways
Southwark & Deptford Tramways
Stamford Hill Tramways
Thanet's Tramways
Victoria & Lambeth Tramways
Waltham Cross & Edmonton Tramways
Walthamstow & Leyton Tramways
Wandsworth & Battersea Tramways

TROLLEYBUS CLASSICS
Croydon's Trolleybuses
Bournemouth Trolleybuses
Maidstone Trolleybuses
Reading Trolleybuses
Woolwich & Dartford Trolleybuses

WATERWAY ALBUMS
Kent and East Sussex Waterways
London's Lost Route to the Sea
London to Portsmouth Waterway
Surrey Waterways

MILITARY BOOKS
Battle over Sussex 1940
Blitz over Sussex 1941-42
Bombers over Sussex 1943-45
Bognor at War
Military Defence of West Sussex
Secret Sussex Resistance

OTHER BOOKS
Betwixt Petersfield & Midhurst
Brickmaking in Sussex
Changing Midhurst
Garraway Father & Son
Index to all Stations
South Eastern & Chatham Railways
London Chatham & Dover Railway

SOUTHERN RAILWAY VIDEO
War on the Line